LEARNING ABOUT DOGS

THE BLOODHOUND

BY CHARLOTTE WILCOX

Consultants:
Myron and Judy Robb
Pine Hollow Bloodhounds

CAPSTONE
HIGH-INTEREST
BOOKS

an imprint of Capstone Press
Mankato, Minnesota

Capstone High-Interest Books are published by Capstone Press
151 Good Counsel Drive, P.O. Box 669, Mankato, Minnesota 56002
http://www.capstone-press.com

Library of Congress Cataloging-in-Publication Data

Wilcox, Charlotte.
The bloodhound/by Charlotte Wilcox.
    p.cm.—(Learning about dogs)
    Includes bibliographical references (p. 45) and index.
    ISBN 0-7368-0761-6
    1. Bloodhound—Juvenile literature. [1. Bloodhound. 2. Dogs. 3. Pets.]
I. Title. II. Series.
SF429.B6 W49 2001
636.753'6—dc21   00-009813

Summary: Discusses the history, development, habits, uses and care of Bloodhounds.

Editorial Credits
Leah K. Pockrandt, editor; Lois Wallentine, product planning editor; Timothy Halldin,
    cover designer and illustrator; Katy Kudela, photo researcher

Photo Credits
Cheryl A. Ertelt, cover, 4, 10, 14, 40–41
Dolly van Zaane, 9, 13, 29, 33, 34
Ginger S. Buck, 37
Jean M. Fogle, 1, 20, 26, 38
Kent and Donna Dannen, 6, 22, 25, 30
Mark Raycroft, 16, 19

1 2 3 4 5 6 06 05 04 03 02 01

TABLE OF CONTENTS

Quick Facts about the Bloodhound

Description

Height: Most Bloodhounds are 25 to 27 inches
(64 to 69 centimeters) tall. Height is
measured from the ground to the withers.
The withers are the tops of the shoulders.

Weight: Most Bloodhounds weigh between
80 and 110 pounds (36 and 50 kilograms).

**Physical
features:**   Bloodhounds are large, heavy dogs with
a good sense of smell. Their skin is loose
and wrinkled around the head and neck.

Color: Bloodhounds can be black and tan, liver and tan, or solid red. Liver is a red-brown color.

Development

Place of origin: Bloodhounds first came to North America from France. Some Bloodhounds later came from England.

History of breed: Bloodhounds descended from large tracking dogs of the Mediterranean region. Roman soldiers brought these dogs to Europe during ancient times.

Numbers: In 1999, the American Kennel Club registered 2,733 Bloodhounds. In 1999, the Canadian Kennel Club registered 57 Bloodhounds. Owners who register their Bloodhounds record their dogs' breeding records with an official club.

Uses: Police and rescue workers use and own Bloodhounds. These workers use the dogs to find people who are missing, on the run, or dead. Some Bloodhounds are family pets.

CHAPTER 1

BEST NOSE IN THE DOG WORLD

Bloodhounds are the largest of the scent hound breeds. Hunters use packs of hounds to chase game such as wild animals or birds. All hound breeds can find and follow animals by scent. This type of hunting is called scent trailing. Hounds trained to scent trail are called scent hounds. Bloodhounds do not catch or attack game. They only chase the game out in the open where a hunter can shoot it.

Scent Hounds
Scent hound breeds range in size from the smallest Beagle to the largest Bloodhound. In between these sizes are Bassets, Coonhounds, Foxhounds, and many other breeds.

Bloodhounds have drooping ears and other physical features common to hound breeds.

All hound breeds share some similarities. Hounds have a howling type of bark called a bay. All scent hounds also have drooping ears.

Bloodhounds use their sense of smell more than other breeds. They can follow the trail of a person or animal even if the trail is several days old. Bloodhounds also can determine detailed information about scents. For example, a trained Bloodhound can tell the direction of a scent trail.

Hunting for People

The Bloodhound's talent for following a trail makes them useful to rescue workers and police. Bloodhounds often help find lost people or property. They also help search for criminals who are hiding or have escaped. Bloodhounds trained for law enforcement or rescue work are never put on the trail of an animal.

Searching for lost or hidden people is called mantrailing. Bloodhounds are better at mantrailing than any other breed. This is because they are the only breed to scent discriminate. They can follow weak scents that other dogs cannot. Once on a trail, Bloodhounds usually will not give up until they find the person or object.

Bloodhounds have a howling type of bark called a bay.

Some people think Bloodhounds are fierce. The idea possibly arose because Bloodhounds have the word blood in their name. Another cause for the idea may be because people usually work Bloodhounds on leashes. Bloodhounds have a habit of lunging toward the people they find. But this movement is not a leap of attack. Some Bloodhounds are trained to leap on a person when they identify the person's scent. Bloodhounds actually are good-natured and seem to enjoy people.

CHAPTER 2

THE BEGINNINGS OF THE BREED

People have used scent-trailing hounds for thousands of years. The first historical reference to dogs similar to Bloodhounds was in Roman times. This period was shortly before A.D. 100. The Roman dogs were slow but excellent trackers. Hunters used them on leashes. The dogs led hunters to the game but did not attack it.

The Roman Empire ruled much of Europe for about 500 years. Roman soldiers lived in camps throughout Europe. These soldiers brought their dogs to the camps. When they left, the soldiers left some dogs behind.

About A.D. 600, people in France crossed the Roman hounds with local breeds. These dogs were very good at scent tracking. They

Bloodhounds use their sense of smell to track animals and people.

became favorites of noblemen and other wealthy people. These people used the dogs to hunt large game such as deer and wild boar.

The Hounds of St. Hubert

Wealthy French noblemen raised and hunted with scent hounds. One such nobleman was François Hubert. He was born about A.D. 656 in the Ardennes area of northern France. He was the son of a French duke. Hubert enjoyed hunting when he was young. He spent much time and money on hunting trips with his friends and hounds.

Two events led Hubert to change his life. One event was the unexpected death of his wife Floribane. The other event happened one day while hunting in the woods near his home. Hubert saw a deer with a shiny cross between its antlers. This vision made him want to become a monk. He gave his money to the poor and went to live in a religious community called a monastery. The monastery was located in the forest region of France. But

For centuries, people used Bloodhounds to hunt a variety of animals.

Hubert did not give up his love of hunting and hunting dogs.

Hubert began raising scent hounds at the monastery. He used dogs raised by his family and friends. These hounds were black and tan. They probably were descendants of the ancient Roman scent hounds.

The Bloodhound's white markings and red color are the result of breeding Hubert's hounds with other breeds.

The Catholic Church named Hubert a saint nearly 100 years after he died. He became the patron saint of hunters in A.D. 825. The monks in his monastery continued raising scent hounds for several hundred years.

The Gentle Hounds

People considered Hubert's hounds valuable. One story says that the monastery used the hounds to pay taxes. Each year, they sent a few hounds to the king of France as payment.

French noblemen used Hubert's hounds to create other breeds. These noblemen mated the hounds with two other hound breeds. One breed was red. The other breed was mostly white. These breeds added the red color and white markings of some modern Bloodhounds.

The result of this breeding was a large, powerful dog with keen scenting ability. The dogs were enthusiastic hunters and easy to handle. The new breed became known as the St. Hubert Hound. People in French-speaking countries still call Bloodhounds St. Hubert Hounds.

St. Hubert Hounds were prized for their friendly personalities and their scenting abilities. Soon, most European kings and noblemen had a pack of St. Hubert Hounds.

CHAPTER 3

THE DEVELOPMENT OF THE BREED

William the Conqueror was a duke in northern France. In 1066, he proclaimed himself king of England. He brought an army to England and took over the government. He also brought his pack of St. Hubert Hounds.

English hunters soon saw the value of the St. Hubert Hounds. Their scenting abilities were better than those of English hounds.

Some hunters wanted a scent dog that would attack. This was useful when hunting large animals. English hunters began to breed St. Hubert Hounds with fiercer English breeds. The dogs produced by these crosses were not as gentle as St. Hubert Hounds.

But many English noblemen wanted to make sure that the gentle St. Hubert breed was not lost. They made sure to mate their St. Hubert

Today's Bloodhounds have the gentle qualities of the St. Hubert Hound.

Hounds only with dogs of the same type and nature. They called their dogs "blooded hounds." This meant they were of pure blood and not crossed with other breeds. Over time, the term blooded hound was shortened to Bloodhound.

An Established Breed

By the 1300s, the Bloodhound was an established breed in England. But this did not happen in France. In the late 1500s, the king of France stopped hunting with St. Hubert Hounds. He liked white hounds better. He started using only white hounds for his hunts.

French noblemen often copied the king's actions. The dark-colored St. Hubert Hounds were no longer popular. The breed died out in France by 1800. But the St. Hubert qualities were preserved in the English Bloodhounds.

Related Breeds

Europe changed during the next few centuries. The forests were cut down to make room for cities and farmland. The large game began to disappear.

Small game animals such as foxes and hares still lived in Europe. People began to hunt these

By the 1800s, the St. Hubert Hound died out in France but was popular in England.

animals for sport. Bloodhounds were not suited for trailing small game. Smaller, faster hounds were needed. But hunters still wanted the Bloodhound's scenting abilities.

Hunters crossed Bloodhounds with smaller dogs to produce Beagles, Harriers, and other small hound breeds. These breeds owe their scenting abilities to Bloodhounds. At the same time, English breeders made sure they kept the pure Bloodhound line intact.

Bloodhounds were first used for search-and-rescue
work in the 1700s in England.

A New Job

English people soon saw that Bloodhounds could
be trained to follow a human scent. They would
not attack the people whom they found. These
qualities were perfect for search work.

Police first started using Bloodhounds for
search work in England during the late 1700s.
They were used to track robbers and other
criminals. The dogs soon proved themselves
to be excellent for this type of work.

Bloodhounds in North America

No one is sure when the first Bloodhounds came to North America. Purebred Bloodhounds have been registered in the United States and Canada since the late 1800s. In the United States, dogs called Bloodhounds were used to track runaway slaves before the Civil War (1861–1865). During the Civil War, they were used in the South to guard prisoners. But these dogs were not true Bloodhounds. They were attack dogs.

Bloodhounds were endangered in England during World War II (1939–1945). There were not enough purebred dogs for breeding. Foxhounds were crossed with a few Bloodhounds. This kept the breed alive until the war ended. After the war, English people received purebred Bloodhounds from North American breeders.

North American dog clubs approve and follow the accepted breed standard for various breeds. The breed standard includes a breed's height, weight, colors, and other features. Judges use the breed standard to judge dogs in shows. The American Kennel Club (AKC) registered 2,733 Bloodhounds in 1999. The Canadian Kennel Club (CKC) registered 57 Bloodhounds in 1999.

CHAPTER 4

THE BLOODHOUND TODAY

Today's Bloodhounds are not hunting dogs. They are too large and slow to be successful hunting dogs. Instead, Bloodhounds mostly are used to find people.

Physical Features

Bloodhounds have a great deal of loose, wrinkled skin around their head and neck. They have long ears, sagging cheeks, and droopy eyes. Some people think this makes them look sleepy, sad, or mean. But most Bloodhounds are playful and gentle.

Bloodhounds have features that are well suited to scent trailing. Their necks are long. The neck muscles stretch easily without becoming tired. This allows the dogs to run with their noses to the ground for long periods

Bloodhounds are large, gentle, and playful dogs.

of time. The Bloodhound's short, smooth coat does not become tangled in weeds or brush.

A Bloodhound travels almost entirely by smell when following a trail. A Bloodhound's loose skin falls down over its eyes when its head is down. This protects the eyes from getting scratched by brush or branches when close to the ground. The skin sometimes almost completely covers the eyes when the dog's nose is down. This does not seem to bother Bloodhounds.

Bloodhound Size

Bloodhounds are large dogs. Males stand between 25 and 27 inches (64 and 69 centimeters) tall. Females stand between 23 and 25 inches (58 and 64 centimeters) tall. Height is measured from the ground to the withers. This area is located at the top of dogs' shoulders.

Bloodhounds also are heavy dogs. Males weigh between 90 and 110 pounds (41 to 50 kilograms). Females weigh about 80 to 100 pounds (36 to 45 kilograms). The larger dogs often are favored in dog shows.

The Bloodhound's loose skin protects the dog's eyes when its head is down.

Bloodhound Colors

Most Bloodhounds are one of three colors or color combinations. Bloodhounds can be black and tan, liver and tan, or solid red. The red color can be dark or light. Some Bloodhounds have a small amount of white on the chest, feet, or tip of the tail.

Police and search-and-rescue teams often use Bloodhounds to find suspects or missing people.

A two-colored Bloodhound has a saddle-shaped marking over the middle of its body. This marking can be black or liver. The marking fades into various shades of tan over the head, chest, feet, and tail. Some Bloodhounds are almost all black with dark red-tan marks only on the face and legs.

Bloodhounds have yellow-brown eyes. Their eye color ranges from light to dark. A Bloodhound's eye color often matches the shade of its coat. Dark-colored Bloodhounds usually have the darkest eyes.

Bloodhounds at Work

Modern Bloodhounds are important in police and search-and-rescue work. This is because they have an uncommon ability to single out one scent. They then direct all their attention to that one scent. Other breeds can get confused when many scents are together.

For mantrailing, the dog starts with a scent from the missing person. This scent can come from footprints or an object that the person has touched. A good scent-trailing Bloodhound can pick up a scent from the air where the person stood. The Bloodhound follows this scent until it finds the person.

Most Bloodhounds work alone with their handler. The handler usually keeps the dog on a leash. The dog may follow a fresh trail quickly. If the trail is older, the dog will need more sniffing time to stay on track. Bloodhounds often forget about everything else when they find a scent trail.

A trained Bloodhound can tell which direction a missing person traveled. If the person crossed a river, a Bloodhound can pick up the scent on the other side. It can follow a scent for many miles without losing the trail.

Missing persons sometimes leave belongings along the trail. Bloodhounds can show police which objects on the trail belonged to the person.

Many people think Bloodhounds are fierce because they catch criminals. But Bloodhounds also find many lost or injured people. They also are good at finding dead bodies after natural disasters or bombings. They are able to scent dead bodies underwater or underground. People also use Bloodhounds to find lost pets and livestock.

Bloodhound Heroes

Nick Carter was a famous Bloodhound from Kentucky. He once picked up the trail of a criminal after four days. He led police to where the criminal was hiding. Bloodhounds have picked up trails that were a week old and still found the person. One Bloodhound led police on a trail for 138 miles (222 kilometers) before finding the criminal.

Bloodhounds can use their trailing abilities after they find people. Bloodhounds that trail suspects can later pick the people out of police

Bloodhounds can follow a scent trail across rivers and can scent dead bodies underwater.

lineups. Police officers believe suspects may have committed crimes. A trained Bloodhound that recognizes a suspect can be used as evidence in a criminal case. A Bloodhound named Jed led his handler for more than 2 miles (3.2 kilometers) during a cold Minnesota winter to find a suspect. Jed later picked the suspect out of a police lineup. Jed's identification helped police charge the suspect with armed robbery. But not all states allow this form of evidence in court.

CHAPTER 5

OWNING A BLOODHOUND

Bloodhounds can make excellent pets. But owners must realize their Bloodhound puppy can grow to weigh 100 pounds (45 kilograms) or more. A Bloodhound puppy may add 5 pounds (2.3 kilograms) and grow 1 inch (2.5 centimeters) in a week.

Living with a Bloodhound

Adult Bloodhounds are large and need plenty of room. Even a well-trained Bloodhound can knock over furniture with a wag of its tail. Their constant drooling also can be a problem. Drool can fly everywhere when a Bloodhound shakes its head.

For centuries, Bloodhounds lived and hunted in packs. Most Bloodhounds are happier in a household where there is another dog.

Bloodhounds need plenty of room both inside and outside.

Bloodhounds can adapt to any type of weather. But Bloodhounds need protection in very cold or hot conditions. Owners should provide Bloodhounds with appropriate shelter such as a doghouse.

Where to Get a Bloodhound

Many people want their first Bloodhound to be a puppy. These people may contact an area Bloodhound club. Clubs help people find good breeders who raise quality dogs.

Breed rescue organizations find homes for homeless dogs. They may offer dogs of all ages for adoption. These dogs usually cost less than one from a breeder. Some adopted dogs even are free. North American Bloodhound clubs offer rescue services for Bloodhounds that need a home.

Keeping a Bloodhound Safe

Bloodhounds cannot be allowed to run unsupervised. Bloodhounds often forget about everything else when they find a scent trail. They may follow a trail for miles or kilometers and completely forget about going

Bloodhounds need a fenced yard so that they can run and not wander out of the yard on a scent trail.

home. Bloodhounds need a fenced yard so they can exercise without getting sidetracked. Outside of the yard, Bloodhounds must be on a leash.

Owners should mark their dogs to identify them if the dogs become lost. Some owners have their telephone number on their dog's collar or tags. Some get their dog tattooed with a patterned mark in the skin. The tattoo is made of tiny ink drops. The tattoo contains an

People may adopt Bloodhounds through a breeder, a Bloodhound club, or a rescue organization.

identification number that will help locate a dog's owner. It is usually placed on the inside of a hind leg.

The microchip is another way to identify dogs. This tiny computer chip is about the size of a grain of rice. A veterinarian surgically inserts the microchip under a dog's skin. It is usually located under the skin on the back of the neck. A veterinarian or shelter worker can scan the microchip if a lost dog is found. The microchip contains the owner's name, address, and telephone number. The microchip also may contain the dog's AKC or CKC registration number.

Feeding a Bloodhound

Bloodhounds need to eat large quantities of food. But Bloodhounds cannot eat too much food at one time. They could get a dangerous stomach problem called bloat or torsion. This condition causes the stomach to fill with gas and become twisted. Dogs can die of bloat.

Owners should divide their Bloodhound's food into two or more meals throughout the day. Owners may want to soak dry dog food in warm water before feeding it to their Bloodhounds.

Bloodhounds also need plenty of water. But they should not drink water or exercise for at least one hour after eating. Drinking or exercising too soon after eating also could cause bloat.

Adult Bloodhounds usually eat about 1 to 2 pounds (.5 to .9 kilogram) of dry kibble or semi-moist dog food each day. The amount of food depends on the dog's age and activity level. Most Bloodhound owners only feed their dog canned dog food as a treat. Some add a little canned food to the daily kibble.

Grooming

Bloodhound owners do not need to provide much care for their dog's short coat. Owners should brush their dog regularly and give it a bath as needed. Owners should give special attention to the long ears and extra folds of skin around the eyes. These areas should be cleaned often to prevent diseases.

Bloodhounds need their teeth cleaned regularly. Owners should use toothpaste made for dogs. Dogs cannot use toothpaste made for people because it must be spit out. Dogs need toothpaste they can swallow. Dogs cannot spit.

Some dogs' toenails get long and must be clipped. Veterinarians can show owners how to perform this grooming task.

Owners must brush their Bloodhounds regularly.

Health Care

Dogs need an annual checkup to guard against diseases. At this medical exam, a veterinarian may give the dog vaccinations. Dogs need these shots of medicine every year to protect them from illness and disease. The veterinarian also may take blood samples to check if the dog has certain diseases.

Bloodhounds have an important job assisting law enforcement officers.

Dogs require special care during warm weather months. During these warm months, dogs need pills to protect them from heartworms. Mosquitoes carry these tiny worms. They enter a dog's heart and slowly destroy it. Dogs also need a yearly checkup for other types of worms.

Owners also must check their Bloodhound's skin for parasites every day during warm weather. These tiny insects include fleas, lice, mites, and ticks. Some ticks carry Lyme disease. This illness can disable or kill an animal or person.

Fleas, lice, and mites also cause problems for dogs. Owners may use flea collars or apply medicine to their dogs to keep these insects away. Owners should use caution and consult a veterinarian before using these products.

Some smaller dog breeds can live 15 years or more. But large dog breeds do not live as long as smaller breeds. A Bloodhound's average life span is about 10 years. As they age, Bloodhounds need special care to keep them in good health.

Bloodhounds have an important place in the modern world. They help rescue workers and police by finding lost people and helping to catch criminals. They also may make people's lives happier through their friendship and affection.

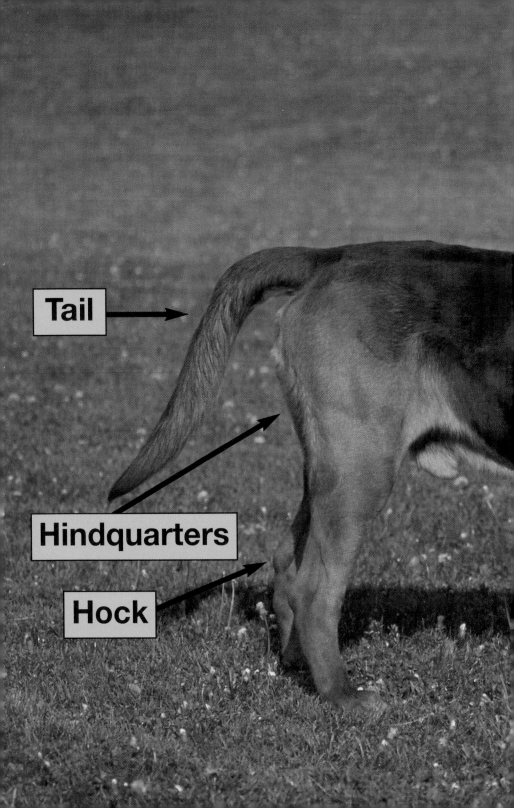

Tail

Hindquarters

Hock

Quick Facts about Dogs

A male dog is called a dog. A female dog is called a bitch. A newborn puppy is called a whelp until it no longer needs its mother's milk. A young dog is called a puppy until it is 1 year old. A family of puppies born at one time is called a litter.

Origin: All dogs, wolves, coyotes, and dingoes descended from a single wolf-like species. People have trained dogs throughout history.

Types: About 350 official dog breeds exist in the world. Dogs can be different sizes and colors. Adult dogs weigh between 2 pounds (.9 kilogram) to more than 200 pounds (91 kilograms). They range from 5 inches (13 centimeters) to 36 inches (91 centimeters) tall.

Reproduction: Most dogs mature between 6 and 18 months. Puppies are born two months after breeding. A female can have two litters per year. An average litter is three to six puppies. Litters of 15 or more puppies are possible.

Development: Whelps are born with their eyes and ears closed. Their eyes and ears open one to two weeks after birth. Whelps try to walk when they are about 2 weeks old. Their teeth begin to come in when they are about 3 weeks old.

Life span: Most dogs are fully grown at 2 years old. With good care, many dogs can live 10 years or longer.

Smell: Dogs have a strong sense of smell. It is many times stronger than a person's sense of smell. Most dogs use their noses more than their eyes and ears. They recognize people, animals, and objects just by smelling them. They may recognize smells from long distances. They also may remember smells for long periods of time.

Hearing: Dogs hear better than people do. Dogs can hear noises from long distances. They also can hear high-pitched sounds that people cannot hear.

Sight: Dogs' eyes are farther to the sides of their heads than people's eyes are. They can see twice as wide around their heads as people can. Most scientists believe that dogs can see some colors.

Touch: Dogs seem to enjoy being petted more than almost any other animal. They also can feel vibrations from approaching trains or the beginnings of earthquakes or storms.

Taste: Dogs do not have a strong sense of taste. This is partly because they swallow food too quickly to taste it well. Dogs prefer certain types of foods. This may be because they like the smell of certain foods better than the smell of other foods.

Navigation: Dogs often can find their way through crowded streets or across miles of wilderness without guidance. This is a special ability that scientists do not fully understand.

Words to Know

bloat (BLOHT)—a condition in which the stomach fills with gas and becomes twisted

Harrier (HAIR-ee-uhr)—a hound originally bred for hunting hares

mantrailing (MAN-tray-ling)—to search for lost or runaway people with dogs

microchip (MYE-kroh-chip)—a computer chip implanted under the skin to identify an animal

monastery (MON-uh-ster-ee)—a group of buildings where monks live and work

register (REJ-uh-stur)—to record a dog's breeding records with an official club

tattoo (ta-TOO)—a word or picture printed onto an animal's skin with ink and needles; owners may have an identification number tattooed on their dogs.

veterinarian (vet-ur-uh-NER-ee-uhn)—a doctor who is trained to diagnose and treat sick or injured animals

To Learn More

American Kennel Club. *The Complete Dog Book for Kids.* New York: Howell Book House, 1996.

Driscoll, Laura. *All about Dogs and Puppies.* All Aboard Books. New York: Grosset & Dunlap, 1998.

Thornton, Kim Campbell. *Bloodhounds: Everything About Purchase, Care, Nutrition, Breeding, Behavior, and Training.* A Complete Pet Owner's Manual. Hauppauge, N.Y.: Barron's, 1998.

Tweedie, Jan. *On the Trail!: A Practical Guide to the Working Bloodhound and Other Search and Rescue Dogs.* Loveland, Colo.: Alpine Publications, 1998.

You can read articles about Bloodhounds in *AKC Gazette, Dog Fancy, Dog and Kennel, Dogs in Canada,* and *Dog World.*

Useful Addresses

American Bloodhound Club
1914 Berry Lane
Daytona Beach, FL 32124

American Kennel Club
5580 Centerview Drive
Raleigh, NC 27606

Canadian Bloodhound Club
4792 Second Line Road
North Lancaster, ON K0C 1Z0
Canada

Canadian Kennel Club
89 Skyway Avenue
Suite 100
Etobicoke, ON M9W 6R4
Canada

National Association for Search and Rescue
4500 Southgate Place
Suite 100
Chantilly, VA 20151-1714

Internet Sites

American Bloodhound Club
http://www.bloodhounds.org

American Kennel Club
http://www.akc.org

The Bloodhound Network
http://www.bloodhounds.com/tbn

Canadian Kennel Club
http://www.ckc.ca

Dogs in Canada
http://www.dogs-in-canada.com

Law Enforcement Bloodhound Association
http://www.leba98.com

National Police Bloodhound Association
http://www.icubed.com/~npba

Index

American Kennel Club (AKC), 21

bloat, 35
blooded hound, 18

Canadian Kennel Club (CKC), 21
Civil War, 21
color, 15, 25–27
Coonhounds, 7
criminal, 8, 20, 28, 39

England, 17, 18, 20, 21
Europe, 11, 18

food, 35, 36
Foxhounds, 7, 21
France, 11, 12, 15, 17, 18

handler, 27, 29
Harriers, 19
heartworms, 38
Hound, St. Hubert, 15, 17–18

insects, 39

Kentucky, 28

Lyme disease, 39

mantrailing, 8, 27
microchip, 34–35
Minnesota, 29

purebred, 21

tattoo, 33

veterinarian, 34, 36, 37, 39

water, 35
William the Conqueror, 17
withers, 24
World War II, 21

48